Prayers
of a

Dedicated
Teacher

Jim Gallery

B̶B

Brighton Books
Nashville, TN

Prayers
— of a
Dedicated
Teacher

Jim Gallery

ISBN 1-58334-119-6

The quoted ideas expressed in this book (but not scripture verses) are not, in all cases, exact quotations, as some have been edited for clarity and brevity. In all cases, the author has attempted to maintain the speaker's original intent. In some cases, quoted material for this book was obtained from secondary sources, primarily print media. While every effort was made to ensure the accuracy of these sources, the accuracy cannot be guaranteed. For additions, deletions, corrections or clarifications in future editions of this text, please write BRIGHTON BOOKS.

All scripture quotations, unless otherwise indicated, are taken from the HOLY BIBLE, NEW INTERNATIONAL VERSION ©. NIV ©. Copyright © 1973, 1978, 1984, by International Bible Society. Used by permission of Zondervan Publishing House. All rights reserved.

Scripture taken from *THE MESSAGE.* Copyright © 1993, 1994,1995,1996. Used by permission of NavPress Publishing Group.

Scripture taken from the NEW AMERICAN STANDARD BIBLE®, Copyright © 1960, 1962, 1963, 1968, 1971, 1972, 1973, 1975, 1977, 1995 by The Lockman Foundation. Used by permission.

Scripture quotations marked (NLT) are taken from The Holy Bible, New Living Translation, Copyright © 1996. Used by permission of Tyndale House Publishers, Incorporated, Wheaton, Illinois 60189. All rights reserved.

Printed in the United States of America
Cover Design & Page Layout: *Bart Dawson*

1 2 3 4 5 6 7 8 9 10 • 01 02 03 04 05 06 07 08 09 10

Acknowledgments: The author is indebted to Criswell Freeman for his support and friendship and to the wonderful staff at Walnut Grove Press.

Dedication...

For First Baptist Church,
Bradenton, Florida,
Ballard Elementary, Walker Junior High,
Manatee High

Table of Contents

Teach Me, Lord:

How to Use This Book

Daily life is a tapestry woven together by the threads of habit. Our habits determine, in part, who we are and who we become. If we develop habits that enrich our lives and the lives of others, we are blessed by God. If, on the other hand, we fall prey to negative thoughts or destructive behavior, we suffer.

No habit is more important to your life than the habit of daily devotion and prayer. But amid the hustle and bustle of the daily grind, prayer and thanksgiving are too often neglected, even by those who know and love God.

This book is intended as a tool for Christian teachers as they develop and reinforce the habit of daily meditation and prayer. If you're already committed to a daily worship time, this book will enrich that experience. If you are not, the simple act of giving God a few minutes each morning will change the tone and direction of your life.

Whether you teach graduate school or Sunday School, whether you lecture at seminary or at Vacation Bible School, you need and deserve a daily conference with the ultimate Teacher. So why not make it a habit to talk things over with Him each day? When you do, you'll enrich the lives of your students as you enrich your own.

"Commit to the Lord whatever you do,
and your plans will succeed."

Proverbs 16:3

Introduction

Teachers come in all shapes and sizes. Some are direct and forceful while others are soft-spoken in style; some teach eloquently from the podium imparting wisdom while others lead the students to exploration and discovery. Some look a lot like our parents, imparting values by word and example; some teachers are friends, and some are employers. Other times, a teacher comes to us in the person of a child.

Each day teachers have countless opportunities to impact the lives of others by what they say and do. But teachers are also students, with the need to learn and grow every day of their lives.

The bookshelves of the world contain many sources of enlightenment, but the ultimate source of true wisdom is God, and we are called upon by Him to study His Word and share His Message. This book celebrates teachers who share God's Message through their words and actions. The pages that follow contain prayers, quotations, stories and Bible verses that demonstrate the power and wisdom that flow through those who teach God's Word. These verses and illustrations are intended to assist dedicated teachers in their efforts to speak the truth—and live it—in such a way that students may experience God's love and His grace.

Teach Me, Lord...
To Know
Your Ways

"Teach me your ways
that I may know you and
find favor with you."

Exodus 33:13

God's ultimate wisdom is revealed to us when we read His word, when we seek His communion in prayer, and when we welcome His love into our hearts. God intends that we worship Him and follow His commandments. When we do, we receive the abundance and joy that He intends for our lives, but to receive His gifts, we must live according to His tenets, not our own.

When God sent His son, Christ Jesus, God bestowed upon mankind the perfect example of sacrificial love. As teachers, we are called upon to mirror Christ's love, not only to our students, but also to the world.

To share God's Message, we must seek His wisdom and his love. We find God's wisdom through the daily study of His Holy Word, and we discover His love when we welcome him into our hearts.

"Just as you do not analyze the words of
someone you love, but accept them
as they are said to you, accept the Word of
Scripture and ponder it in your heart."

Dietrich Bonhoeffer

"The Bible is God's Word, given to us by God
Himself so we can know Him and
His will for our lives."

Billy Graham

"The Scriptures were not given for
our information, but for our transformation."

D. L. Moody

Today's Prayer

$\mathcal{L}$ord, teach me Your ways.
The conventional wisdom of the
world is seldom Your wisdom.
Give me discernment for Your truth.
May You find me a faithful teacher of
Your Word to students who will in turn
pass on that truth to others.

Amen

2

Teach Me, Lord...
To Live by
Your Word

"...to teach you that man does not live by bread alone but on every word that comes from the mouth of the Lord."

Deuteronomy 8:3

God gave us His Word that we might know His will. As we read His scriptures, we must choose how we will respond to His commandments: Will we use God's word to guide our actions, or will we chart a different course, one restricted by our own limitations and weaknesses?

God's word is a shining beacon, a touchstone for the lives of those who live according to His tenets. When we approach the Bible with a sense of awe and with a determination to live according to God's laws, we invite untold blessings into our lives. Only then can we fulfill God's ultimate plan for our lives and help others do the same.

As Christian teachers, we are called not only to share God's Message, but to live it. When that Message comes alive within us, then we, too, become shining beacons for students to follow.

"If I obey Jesus Christ in the seemingly
random circumstances of life, they
become pinholes through which I see
the face of God."

Oswald Chambers

"If my life is surrendered to God,
all is well. Let me not grab it back,
as though it were in peril in His hand
but would be safer in mine!"

Elisabeth Elliot

"Nobody ever outgrows Scripture;
the book widens and deepens
with our years."

C. H. Spurgeon

"Prayer is God's provision for us to know Him,
to know His purposes and His ways,
to experience His mighty presence
working in us and through us to accomplish
His perfect will."

Henry Blackaby

Today's Prayer

*L*ord, Your Word is a lamp unto my feet
and a light unto my path. I seek to become a
faithful student and teacher of Your Word,
but I know I must also be a "doer"
of the Word. As I study Your teachings,
and as those teachings become
an ever-growing part of my being,
guide me, Lord, in the way that
You would have me go, and use
me according to Your plan that I may
help others experience Your glory
and Your love.

Amen

3

Teach Me, Lord...
To Be a
Worthy Example to
My Students

"...teach them to your children,
talking about them when you sit at
home and when you walk along the
road, when you lie down and
when you get up."
Deuteronomy 11:19 NIV

A teacher is always a teacher, inside the classroom and out. Sometimes the lessons learned outside the classroom are the most important lessons of all.

Before I was born I was enrolled in Sunday School. Our church encouraged expectant mothers to "train up a child in the way he should go" by attending prenatal classes and making sure the baby was started off properly in Sunday School. Mom attended, and so did I.

I know my childhood Sunday School teachers were dedicated and godly persons, but I remember little of what they said. Like most young boys, I was much better at observing my teachers than I was at listening to their words. One of my most memorable teachers was Charlie Johnson, a big man filled with a joy for life and a love for the church. I am certain that he taught me about Jesus in Sunday School, but I don't remember what Charlie said. I do, however, have a crystal-clear memory of the things that Charlie did.

Charlie Johnson took us on camping trips and to amusement parks. He organized parties and Bible studies. On weekends Charlie always seemed to have something planned; in short, he kept us out of trouble and

kept us involved in the church, all the while showing us the love of Christ. Sunday School was then, and is now, a place where I feel at home, thanks in large part to Charlie.

Was Charlie Johnson unique? Did he possess unequaled skills in the classroom? Was he a great orator or an heir to a family fortune that left him with no responsibilities and endless free time? None of the above. Charlie was simply an enthused, dedicated Sunday School teacher. He, like countless others, was willing to do God's work here on earth by letting the joy of Christ shine through him. God Bless Charlie Johnson and all the other Christian men and women whose actions speak—and preach—louder than words.

"Preach the gospel every day;
    if necessary, use words."

St. Francis of Assisi

"God uses ordinary people who are
    obedient to him to do extraordinary things."

John Maxwell

Today's Prayer

*L*ord, Help me always to show my
concern for my students, not only
in the classroom, but also outside it.
May the words of truth I share with
my students be the same words of truth
that guide my life. Thank You, Lord,
for the opportunity to express my love
and concern for my students
through words and deeds.

Amen

4

Teach Me, Lord...
To Share With
My Students What is
Good and Right

"...I will teach you the way that is
good and right."

I Samuel 12:23

God's laws are without flaw. If only the same could be said for those of us who must try our best to live by them. We are imperfect people living in an imperfect world, struggling day by day to do the good and right thing. Sometimes, we fall short.

As teachers, we are imperfect, but our message is not. God's laws were laid down with the foundation of the universe, and they remain as flawless today as they were the instant He created them. Our task is straightforward: to share God's perfect message with an imperfect world.

Christian teachers have a special responsibility to share the good news of Jesus Christ. His message is good and right, now and forever. Amen.

"Your heavenly Father is too good to be
unkind and too wise to make mistakes."

C. H. Spurgeon

"Let him who wants a true church cling to
the Word by which everything is upheld."

Martin Luther

"The great need of the hour among persons
spiritually hungry is twofold:
First, to know the Scriptures, apart from
which no saving truth will be vouchsafed by our
Lord; the second, to be enlightened by
the Spirit, apart from whom the Scriptures
will not be understood."

A. W. Tozer

Today's Prayer

*L*ord, you are perfect and absolutely good. Yet You have chosen an imperfect vessel such as myself to teach others of Your goodness. Help me, Lord, to share Your perfect Message to an imperfect world. May I be found to be a good and faithful servant, and may others see through my own imperfections so that they might gaze upon You and experience Your perfect love.

Amen

5

Teach Me, Lord...
To Allow You to
Guide My Ways

> "I will instruct you and teach you in
> the way you should go…"
>
> *Psalm 32:8*

Someone once said that Christopher Columbus would have landed at his intended destination of North America if only he had stopped and asked for directions. But, being a man, he couldn't bring himself to ask for help and guidance.

If we are to be successful in our endeavors, we must seek direction from the ultimate source; we must look to God for His perfect guidance.

I enjoy white water rafting trips on the Ocoee River in East Tennessee. These adventures satisfy my thirst for "the thrill of victory and the agony of defeat," but there are limits to my spirit of conquest. I choose to shoot the rapids only when accompanied by a seasoned guide. With the guide in charge, I know that we will avoid whirlpools, boulders, bears and snakes. With the guide in charge, I feel secure, and I can fully enjoy the ride.

Life's journey is not unlike the Ocoee River. Sometimes the waters are calm, but, sooner rather than later, we encounter powerful rapids, the storm clouds rise, and we need guidance. It seems reasonable to call upon the Guide who has seen every problem we will ever face. It seems reasonable to call upon the Guide who loves us and wants the best for us. That Guide, of course, is God, and with Him at the helm, we have absolutely nothing to fear.

"Look for yourself and you will find in the
long run only hatred, loneliness, despair,
rage, ruin and decay. But look for Christ and
you will find Him, and with Him
everything else thrown in."

C. S. Lewis

"Lord, I am no longer my own, but Yours.
Put me to what You will, rank me with
whom You will. Let me be employed by You or
laid aside for You, exalted for You or
brought low by You. Let me have all things,
let me have nothing, I freely and heartily
yield all things to Your pleasure and disposal.
And now, O glorious and blessed God, Father,
Son, and Holy Spirit, You are mine and
I am Yours. So be it. Amen."

John Wesley

Today's Prayer

*L*ord, Thank You for giving me the miraculous gift of life. Thank You for the adventures of life, the ups and downs, the joys and sorrows. Guide me, Lord, on my journey, and show me the way You would have me go. I know that I can never face any danger that You have not already met and conquered. I know that You love me more than I love myself. May I search Your word and listen to Your voice every day that I live.

Amen

6

Teach Me, Lord...
To Be a
Witness

"Then will I teach transgressors
your ways, and sinners will
turn back to you."

Psalm 51:13

God calls upon his people to be witnesses to the world, and teachers are no exception. The most effective teachers share the good news through their words *and* actions.

She taught both my daughter and son in elementary school. In all academic aspects she was a good teacher, but it was the spiritual concern she showed for her students that set her apart. At the beginning of the school year, she would ask every parent if they had any objections to her sharing a Bible story each day. Fortunately for my children, no parents objected, so this teacher was able to prepare her students both academically and spiritually.

When my son invited Jesus into his heart, a baptism was planned. Our church did not have a baptistry so we scheduled an afternoon service at a neighbor church. Fellow church members attended the second church service of the day, and I was thankful. As I looked out at the congregation, I saw a welcome guest: my son's teacher. She sat through the service with misty eyes and thanksgiving in her heart. After the service, she confided to me that my son was her 6th student to become a Christian. My eyes, too, became misty as I thanked her for coming. In my heart I thanked God for a teacher who cared about the wholeness of my children.

"The wise Christian will watch for opportunities to do good, to speak the life-bringing word to sinners, to pray the rescuing prayer of intercession."

A. W. Tozer

"God of our life, there are days when the burdens we carry chafe our shoulders and weigh us down; when the road seems dreary and endless, the skies grey and threatening; when our lives have no music in them, and our hearts are lonely, and our souls have lost their courage. Flood the path with light, run our eyes to where the skies are full of promise; tune our hearts to brave music; give us the sense of comradeship with heroes and saints of every age; and so quicken our spirits that we may be able to encourage the souls of all who journey with us on the road of life, to Your honour and glory."

St. Augustine

Today's Prayer

*L*ord, I thank You today for the opportunity to teach and to witness and to share the good news of Your Message. Help me to be an influence for good in the lives of my students. Lord, help me to care for the whole student. Help me to be sensitive to the needs of each of those I teach, and use me, Lord, as Your tool to draw my students closer to You.

Amen

7

Teach Me, Lord...
To Live
Wisely

"Oh Teach us to live well! Teach us
to live wisely and well."
Psalm 90:12 (The Message)

Teachers who wish to leave a lasting legacy must not only share great ideas and lessons, they must also make wise personal choices outside the classroom. When a student observes a teacher whose words and deeds are in harmony, the student respects the teacher *and* the message.

My pastor, Dr. Tom McCoy, is an engaging teacher and a powerful voice from the pulpit. Tom speaks with authority, in large part, because of the way he conducts his life. Tom's daily walk with God is his best sermon illustration.

When Tom talks about tithing, his congregation knows that Tom, too, tithes. When he talks about family matters, the congregation knows Tom to be a loving and faithful father. When he speaks on the topic of love, his congregation knows Tom to be a caring husband and a faithful friend. When Tom talks about God, the congregation knows of Tom's dedication and discipleship. Tom doesn't simply teach from the Bible, he lives it.

If we are to be effective teachers in service of God, we must not only share the good news of God's word, we must also live according to God's principles. If we are to serve our students, we must not only lecture wisely, we must also live wisely.

"Don't worry about what you do not
understand.... Worry about what you do
understand in the Bible but do not live by."

Corrie ten Boom

"The alternative to discipline is disaster."

Vance Havner

"There may be no trumpet sound or
loud applause when we make a right decision,
just a calm sense of resolution and peace. "

Gloria Gaither

Today's Prayer

*L*ord, I humbly acknowledge
how much easier it is to teach lessons
than it is to live by them. But I know,
Lord, that I must not only teach Your
Word, I must also seek to live it. I know
that a well-lived life gives my message
meaning and credibility and impact.
Help me to practice what I teach.
May I impart Your great truths to
students who observe in my actions
a commitment to the wise and
Godly life.

Amen

8

Teach Me, Lord...
To Please
You

"Teach me how to live to please you,
because you are my God…"
Psalm 143:10a (The Message)

There is always someone to please. We try to please our families, our employers, our coworkers, our coaches and our friends. In many cases, our efforts to please are helpful and good, but pleasing others should always be of secondary importance. We must first seek to please God.

The apostle Paul writes that he is not concerned by the opinions of others or even by the way he judges himself. Paul writes that he is only concerned with the judgement of the Lord (*1 Corinthians 4:2-4*). In a letter to Timothy, Paul explains that a good soldier only wants to please the one who enlisted him (*1 Timothy 2:5*), and those words apply to our lives as well. If we are to be good soldiers in God's service, we must first seek His will and His approval. The God who has given us everything deserves nothing less.

"Let us remember therefore this lesson:
That to worship our God sincerely we must
evermore begin by hearkening to His voice,
and by giving ear to what He commands us.
For if every man goes after his own way,
we shall wander. We may well run, but we shall
never be a whit nearer to the right way,
but rather farther away from it."

John Calvin

"Whether we think of, or speak to, God,
whether we act or suffer for Him,
all is prayer, when we have no other object
than His love, and the desire of pleasing Him."

John Wesley

Today's Prayer

Lord, You have created me and
given me a purpose. Help me always
to seek to please You in every aspect of
my life. As I teach my students, may I
bring You pleasure in all that I say and
do. And Lord, help me to feel Your
pleasure as I do Your will.

Amen

9

Teach Me, Lord...
To Pray

> "One day Jesus was praying in a
> certain place. When he finished,
> one of his disciples said to him,
> 'Lord, teach us to pray.'"
>
> *Luke 11:1*

The scripture instructs us to make daily prayer a high priority. Most of us don't question the need for prayer, but like the disciples, we may want to learn more about *how* to pray.

As a child I went to church every Sunday. Like most children of my age, I possessed a short attention span: Long sermons and opera-style solos tended to cause my eyelids to gain weight. However, when prayer time came and Charlie Elmore was called upon to lead us, I came alive.

Charlie didn't use thee's and thou's, and he didn't follow a formula when he prayed. Charlie never prayed the same phrase over and over again like some in our church. Instead, he prayed like he was really talking to God. Furthermore, when Charlie prayed, I had the distinct impression that it hadn't been too long since he had last spoken with God. Charlie would squeeze his Bible tightly and hold it close to his chest. Most of those who prayed at our church bowed their heads, but Charlie Elmore, with eyes squinted shut, would lift his head and prayers toward heaven.

I once asked Charlie the secret to effective prayer. He thought for a short moment and replied there was no secret. He said that he just prayed often, that he prayed from the heart, and that he left the rest up to God.

Good books have been written on prayer; good sermons have been preached about prayer; good songs have been sung on prayer; but the best way to learn about prayer is simple…just pray. Pray early and often, and leave the rest up to your heavenly Father.

"Never say you will pray about a thing;
pray about it."

Oswald Chambers

"Our prayers may be very beautiful in
appearance and might appear to be the
very paragon of devotion, but unless there is
a secret spiritual force in them, they are
vain things."

C. H. Spurgeon

"Don't pray when you feel like it;
make an appointment with the King
and keep it."

Corrie ten Boom

Today's Prayer

*L*ord, as I seek to teach others,
I know that I must be a person of
prayer. I know that I must pray
without ceasing, Lord, because it is
through constant prayer that I can
discover Your will for my life.
Help me to come to You often
with the concerns of my heart.
May I seek You and only You
with my praise and petition.

Amen

10

Teach Me, Lord...
To Allow the
Holy Spirit
to Guide Me

"But the Counselor, the Holy Spirit,
whom the Father will send in my
name, will teach you all things and
will remind you of everything I have
said to you."

John 14:26

God seeks to fill us with His Spirit, but He does not force the Holy Sprit upon us. God allows his children to choose for themselves whether to quench the Spirit or give Him free reign in their lives.

Jesus calls upon us to accept the Holy Spirit into our lives (*John 3:5-6*). When we do, we are transformed and reborn. But a one-time acquaintance with the Holy Spirit is not what God has planned for us—God's designs are much grander than that. He desires that we discover the joys of *daily* communion with His Holy Spirit.

As teachers, we must seek not only the will of God, but also the life-changing spirit of God. When we find both, we transform not only ourselves, but also our students.

"It may be said without qualification that
every man is as holy and as full of the Spirit
as he wants to be. He may not be as full as
he wishes he were, but he is most certainly as
full as he wants to be."

A. W. Tozer

"The Holy Spirit is like electricity;
He won't come in unless He can get out."

Billy Graham

"When the witness and the fruit of the
Spirit meet together, there can be
no stronger proof that we are of God."

John Wesley

Today's Prayer

*L*ord, You have blessed me with
the gift of Your Holy Spirit.
Help me to always welcome that
gift into my heart. And help me, Lord,
to be a daily witness to the glory and
the power that Your Spirit brings to
my life. Let me share the good news
of Your gifts with family, friends,
students, and the world. And let the
meditations of my heart be worthy
of the Holy Spirit that You have sent
to fill my soul.

Amen

11

Teach Me, Lord...
To Encourage
My Students

"And let us consider how we may
spur one another on toward love
and good deeds....let us encourage
one another..."

Hebrews 10:24,25

All of God's children were created with gifts and talents to be used for God's work. Teachers have the privilege of helping their students discover those gifts; Christian teachers help their students dedicate those gifts to God.

The church at Ephesus received written instruction from Paul regarding the proper way to speak to one another: "Watch the way you talk…Say only what helps, each word a gift." (*Ephesians 4:29 The Message*). Thoughtful Christian teachers make their words like gifts to their students, understanding that encouraging words can help a student reach his or her potential in the Lord.

One school administration decided to run an experiment. A class of underachievers and a class of overachievers were assigned to equally talented teachers. The teacher with the overachieving class was told he had the underachievers. The underachieving class was placed with a teacher who was told he had the overachievers. At the end of the year the underachievers had become the overachievers and the overachievers the underachievers. The students' scholarship rose and fell according to the expectations of their teachers.

56

Teachers' expectations tend to become reality in the classroom and beyond. Wise teachers understand this fact and create expectations of success. Those who find creative ways to encourage their students improve grades and lives, but not necessarily in that order.

"Since you cannot do good to all, you are to pay special regard to those who, by the accidents of time, or place, or circumstances, are brought into closer connection with you."

St. Augustine

"Encouragement is the oxygen of the soul."

John Maxwell

"A lot of people have gone further than they thought they could because someone else thought they could."

Zig Ziglar

Today's Prayer

*L*ord, thank You for all my students.
Use me according to Your desires
to help them discover their gifts.
And help me, Lord, to encourage
every student in the classroom, so that
the words of my mouth will be
a gift to all those I teach.

Amen

12

Teach Me, Lord...
To Share a
True Message

> "You must teach what is in accord
> with sound doctrine."
> *Titus 2:1*

We live in a world filled with messages, many of which are untrue. Advertisers encourage us to seek pleasure and profit; the media encourages us to imitate unhealthy role models; our peers tempt us to keep up with the Joneses. We are told that more is better and that happiness can be bought. These messages originate in the heart of fallible men, not in the Word of God.

Through His Holy Word, God shares a *true* message, one that is quite different form the messages that the world teaches. God's Message centers around the life, death, and resurrection of His son Jesus, who sacrificed His own earthly existence for our eternal salvation. God's Message includes a promise of His love, a love that is everlasting. God has a grand and glorious plan for each of us, but to fully realize the richness that God intends for our lives, we must live in the light of his divine truth.

Jesus says, "To this end was I born, and for this cause came I into the world, that I should bear witness unto the truth." *(John 18:37 KJV)* As teachers, we, too, have a responsibility to share a message that is consistent with God's Word. When we discover that message and teach it, we make a lasting mark upon our students and upon the world.

"Anything that comes to us from the God of
the Word will deepen our love for the
Word of God."

A. W. Tozer

"The stars may fall, but God's promises will
stand and be fulfilled."

J. I. Packer

"We have ample evidence that the Lord is
able to guide. The promises cover every
imaginable situation. All we need to do is to
take the hand He stretches out.

Elisabeth Elliot

Today's Prayer

Lord, thank You for Your love and for a Message that is holy and true. Help me to discern right from wrong in a world that seeks to hide the difference between the two. And help me to share Your Message, Lord, with my students as I live according to Your Word.

Amen

13

Teach Me, Lord...
To Realize
My Awesome
Responsibility

"Don't be in any rush to become
a teacher, my friends. Teaching is
highly responsible work. Teachers are
held to the strictest standards."
James 3:1 (The Message)

When we become Christian teachers, we shoulder a heavy burden — thankfully, God stands willing, ready, and perfectly able to help us carry that load. We, as teachers, must do our part by sharing faithfully God's good news and by living according to His laws; the rest is up to Him.

Christian teachers, whether they realize it or not, form an important partnership with God. That partnership represents a profound responsibility. Spiritual lives hang in the balance. But be comforted: Even when we humans falter, God is up to the task.

"If a teacher fascinates with his doctrine,
his teaching never came from God. The
teacher who came from God is the one who
clears the way for Jesus and keeps it clear.
Oswald Chambers

"Seeing that a Pilot steers the ship in which
we sail, who will never allow us to perish
even in the midst of shipwrecks, there is no
reason why our minds should be overwhelmed
with fear and overcome with weariness."
John Calvin

"O Love ever burning and never
extinguished...my God, set me on fire."
St. Augustine

Today's Prayer

---

*L*ord, I know that my role as
a teacher is an awesome responsibility.
Help me to always be mindful of that
responsibility and help me, Lord, to do
Your will as I teach and minister to my
students. Use me to do Your will, Lord,
and help me to be a force for good in
the classroom as I reflect Your care
and Your love.

Amen

14

Teach Me, Lord...
To Have a
Servant Heart

"Now that I, your Lord and Teacher,
have washed your feet, you also
should wash one another's feet. I
have set an example that you should
do as I have done for you. I tell you
the truth, no servant is greater than
his master, nor is a messenger
greater than the one who sent him."

John 13:14-16

As teachers, we are leaders of the classroom, but as Christians, we are called upon to be servants; in point of fact, we are both. As Christian leaders, God instructs us to shepherd our flock with care ("...if it is leadership, let him govern diligently..." *Romans 12:8*). As servants, we must put the flock's needs above our own (*Matthew 23:11*).

When we lead our students with a servant's heart, we follow the word of God. By doing so, we model the actions of our savior Jesus Christ who so readily and humbly served those who followed Him.

"Do all the good you can, by all means you can,
in all the places you can, at all the times
you can, to all the people you can,
as long as ever you can."

John Wesley

"In God's family, there is to be one great body
of people: servants. In fact, that's the way
to the top in his kingdom."

Chuck Swindoll

"Have thy tools ready; God will find thee work."

Charles Kingsley

Today's Prayer

*L*ord, help me always to have
the heart of a servant. Let me follow
the example of Your Son by serving
others gladly, and let me never fall prey
to feelings of resentment, anger, or
mistrust. Lord, Your Word promises that
You have a grand purpose for my life.
Let me discover Your purpose and
follow Your will as I lead a life of
service to others.

Amen

15

Teach Me, Lord...
To Be
Obedient

"...and teaching them to obey
everything I have commanded you.
And surely I am with you always, to
the very end of the age."
Matthew 28:20

We human beings share a common trait: we are headstrong. We prefer to make our own plans and have our own way. But our way is not always God's way, and when our plans come in conflict with God's, we invite trouble and pain into our lives.

God's laws are clearly established through the teachings of His Holy Word, but we mortals face powerful temptations to disobey. God understands the human tendency toward disobedience…after all, He first encountered it in the Garden of Eden. But God also understands that His way is the good and right path for our lives, so He asks us to be obedient to Him, and He rewards us when we are.

Just as teachers expect obedience from their students, so should teachers be obedient to the One who laid the foundation of the universe.

"It is human to err; it is devilish to
remain willfully in error."

St. Augustine

"Only he who believes is obedient.
Only he who is obedient believes."

Dietrich Bonhoeffer

"When we choose deliberately to obey Him,
then He will tax the remotest star and
the last grain of sand to assist us with all His
almighty power."

Oswald Chambers

Today's Prayer

Lord, help me this day to follow
Your will and obey Your Word. I am
weak in so many ways, Lord, and my
understanding is so limited that I
must depend upon You. Help me to
resist the temptations of this world as
I set my gaze on the next, and help me
to obey Your commandments today
and forever.

Amen

16

Teach Me, Lord...
That Learning
is Forever

"Instruct a wise man and he will be
wiser still; teach a righteous man
and he will add to his learning."
Proverbs 9:9

Learning is not a one-time event, it is a process. And for the wise and the righteous, the learning process lasts a lifetime.

Ron Medlin is an experienced teacher of English and English Literature. He teaches his subject well, but he teaches more than words on a page. As a result, Ron has a file cabinet full of letters from former students thanking him not only for lessons in English but also for his lessons about life. Ron shares the message that learning can and should be a lifetime journey. The same theory applies to the well-lived Christian life.

A Christian's education is never completed. There is always more to learn about God's Word and His will. As we continue to study the Bible and seek God's wisdom, we grow as teachers and, more importantly, as earthly servants of God.

"Knowledge is power."

Francis Bacon

"Education without religion, as useful as it is,
seems rather to make man a more clever devil."

C. S. Lewis

"Be assiduous in reading the Holy Scriptures.
This is the fountain whence all knowledge in
divinity must be derived. Therefore let not this
treasure lie by you neglected."

Jonathan Edwards

Today's Prayer

*L*ord, I want to teach my subject well, but more importantly, I want to teach my students well. Help me to inspire those whom I teach to become lifelong seekers of knowledge and lifelong students of Your Word. May my passion for learning become their passion for learning, and may my passion for Your Word be clearly reflected to those whom I teach.

Amen

17

Teach Me, Lord...
To Provide
Discipline

"The fear of the Lord is the
beginning of knowledge, but fools
despise wisdom and discipline."

Proverbs 1:7

Learning can only take place in a disciplined environment. A teacher must create that environment if the student is to learn. Discipline is not always comfortable nor is it always pleasant, but the wise teacher knows that it is necessary for effective learning to take place.

My sister Jan began her sixth-grade year with fear and trepidation. Her teacher, Jim Kronus, began his relationship with students by "laying down the law." From Jan's perspective, Mr. Kronus was tough, and she worried that the year would be unpleasant. Much to my sister's surprise, it was Jan's best year ever. Why? Because of discipline.

Early on, her teacher had established discipline in the classroom, thus freeing each student to learn in a calm, structured environment. While some teachers were dealing with students who were unruly and rebellious, Jim Kronus had settled that issue at the beginning of the school year.

God's Word warns of the dangers associated with undisciplined behavior. Young students in particular are at risk when they are allowed to behave irresponsibly. As Christian leaders, we are called upon to establish a disciplined environment for the children who fall under our care.

"God does not discipline us to subdue us, but
to condition us for a life of usefulness
and blessedness."

Billy Graham

"Among the enemies to devotion none is
so harmful as distractions. Whatever excites
the curiosity, scatters the thoughts, disquiets
the heart, absorbs the interests or shifts our life
focus from the kingdom of God within us to the
world around us — that is a distraction;
and the world is full of them."

A. W. Tozer

"I've never met anyone who became instantly
mature. It's a painstaking process that God takes
us through, and it includes such things as waiting,
failing, losing, and being misunderstood — each
calling for extra doses of perseverance."

Chuck Swindoll

Today's Prayer

*L*ord, thank You for the opportunity to lead students in the paths of wisdom and knowledge. Grant that their learning experiences will be fruitful. Help me, Lord, to provide leadership in my classroom, and show me ways to establish discipline while mirroring Your love.

Amen

18

Teach Me, Lord...
To Let You
Guide My
Speech

"A wise man's heart guides his
mouth and his lips promote
instruction."

Proverbs 16:23

God promises to guide the speech of his followers. His son Jesus assures us that even when we stand before rulers, the Holy Spirit will teach what is to be said (*Luke 12:11,12*). Thus, when we commit our hearts to God, we find it easier to speak words that are pleasing to Him.

I was the last person to sign up as a chaperone for a youth trip to Gatlinburg, Tennessee, and, not surprisingly, I found myself with the toughest assignment: behaviorally challenged teenage boys. I quickly became aware of my challenge when a youngster named David decided to go down a Super Slide despite the fact that the slide was closed to the public and covered with a thin sheet of ice. When David finally came to a stop half a block from the slide, he left broken fences and acquired a few broken bones. Such was my challenge, and it was only day one.

The leading member of the group was a boy named Larry. Larry appeared totally disinterested in the spiritual reasons for the trip; he seemed much more interested in causing minor disturbances and petty property damage. That's why I was quite surprised on the night Larry asked me to talk with him about religion. We found a quiet place and Larry started asking serious questions. Soon, I found myself quoting scripture. Several times during the hour-long discussion, I felt that God gave me scripture verses to share with the teenager.

Still, I wasn't sure that I was making a difference. But three weeks later, Larry accepted Christ as his Savior.

A few days after Larry had made his decision, we talked. I learned that our discussion in Gatlinburg had been a turning point in Larry's spiritual life. I looked back and marveled at the way God had given me the right words to help shape a young man's eternal destiny.

"A saint's life is in the hands of God as a bow and arrow in the hands of an archer. God is aiming at something the saint cannot see."

Oswald Chambers

"God walks with us. . . . He scoops us up in His arms or simply sits with us in silent strength until we cannot avoid the awesome recognition that yes, even now, He is there."

Gloria Gaither

Today's Prayer

*L*ord, thank You for guiding my speech. Let my heart be pure, and make my words a clear reflection of Your will. I thank You that in the classroom, I am guided in word and deed by an all-knowing God. Use my words to accomplish Your will in the lives of my students so that they, too, may share Your glorious Message.

Amen

19

Teach Me, Lord...
To Be a
Worthy Example

"Follow my example, as I follow the
example of Christ. I praise you for
remembering me in everything and
for holding to the teachings, just as
I passed them on to you."

1 Corinthians 11:1,2

Students *listen* to their teachers occasionally, but they *watch* their teachers obsessively. In the classroom, as in life, actions speak in stentorian tones while words seldom rise above a whisper. The life of a teacher will validate—or invalidate—the words that the teacher speaks.

My niece, Tori Bell, was very impressed with her math teacher, Mrs. Beebe. Mrs. Beebe did a wonderful job communicating numbers, formulas, and ideas, but Tori was more impressed with the teacher's positive outlook on life. Somehow Tori had become aware of personal struggles her teacher faced. These struggles impressed Tori as significant and difficult. Yet, day after day, Mrs. Beebe exuded optimism and determination as she encouraged every student in the classroom.

Of course, every teacher must do his or her best to master the course material. But, ultimately, subject matter is less important than the teacher who teaches it. Teachers who demonstrate optimism, courage, and faith make lasting impressions on their students because the students may not be listening, but they are *always* watching.

"You can never separate a leader's actions
from his character."

John Maxwell

"Leadership requires vision, and whence will
vision come except from hours spent in the
presence of God in humble and fervent prayer?"

A. W. Tozer

"Kids go where there is excitement.
They stay where there is love."

Zig Ziglar

Today's Prayer

*L*ord, always give me joy and passion
for the teaching of Your Word. Help me
to prepare myself when I teach, and
help me understand that my preparation
is more than knowledge, it is also
attitude. Help me also to live
successfully in Your will, so that
I might be a worthy example to others.
May my words be authenticated by
my actions, this day and every day.

Amen

20

Teach Me, Lord...
To Equip My
Students with
Your Word

"All scripture is God-breathed and is
useful for teaching, rebuking,
correcting and training in
righteousness so that the man of
God may be thoroughly equipped
for every good work."

2 Timothy 3:16,17

In some circles, it is not politically correct to believe in absolutes. We live in a world in which words like "honesty" and "character" have become out-dated terms for those who seek to circumvent the immutable laws handed down in God's Word. But absolutes do exist. God has given His people absolute truths in the form of His scripture, and His Words teach us and guide us through life.

Paul tells his student Timothy that God's Word is alive. Scripture is relevant to our daily lives because it leads us along the path that God has planned for us. God's Word has the power to teach us, to rebuke us, to correct us, and to save us.

The absolute truth handed down by God gives us purpose and protection. God's chosen teachers share the absolute truth of His Word with their students, and they share the message that a life without truth is like a rudderless ship: adrift and in peril.

"If you believe what you like in the Gospel,
   and reject what you don't like, it is not the
      Gospel you believe, but yourself."

St. Augustine

"You should not believe your conscience and
   your feelings more than the word which the
   Lord who receives sinners preaches to you."

Martin Luther

"The promises of Scripture are not mere pious
   hopes or sanctified guesses. They are more
   than sentimental words to be printed on
   decorated cards for Sunday School children.
   They are eternal verities. They are true.
   There is no perhaps about them."

Peter Marshall

Today's Prayer

Lord, teach me Your absolutes.
When necessary, correct me of wrong
thinking. May Your Word guide me in
teaching righteousness to my students.
Thank You, Lord, for the absolute
truths that anchor Your believers in a
world that is so often adrift in confusion.
May my teaching reflect a steadfast
belief in Your Word.

Amen

21

Teach Me, Lord...
To Work
Diligently

"Whatever you do, work at it with
all your heart, as working for the
Lord, not for men...."
Colossians 3:23

The Bible teaches the value of hard work. God-centered work is not punishment, it is part of the purpose for which we were created.

Charles Quarmby became the band director at the local high school when I was a sixth grader. He also was my next-door neighbor. Until Mr. Quarmby moved next door, I had been preparing for a glorious football career. I dreamed of Friday night games, Saturday afternoon tackles, and, just maybe, Sunday afternoon touchdowns.

These dreams came to a screeching halt when I met Mr. Quarmby. He sized me up and said, "You have trombone lips." If God had wanted me to be a football player, I reasoned, he would have made me fast or strong. Instead He gave me trombone lips. So began my career in the band.

Charles Quarmby ran a tight ship. He was serious about our "bandsmanship." Our rehearsals were hard work and practice time was never a time for "goofing off." Through all the hard work, one fact always kept me going: Our band went to the state contest every year.

Under the firm direction of Charles Quarmby, and through the dint of our own efforts, we became one of the best bands in the entire state of Florida. We earned *invitations to out-of-state events, and we felt pride in our accomplishments. I learned from Mr. Quarmby that talent is almost never as important as hard work. And I learned that a job well done is its own reward.*

The Lord did not design his people to be mediocre; He created us to do good work, to do His work, and to reap the benefits for ourselves and for others. When we work diligently in God's service, He rewards us—now and eternally.

"Natural abilities are like natural plants;
they need pruning by study."

Francis Bacon

"We trust as if it all depended on God, and
work as if it all depended on us."

C. H. Spurgeon

"Work, work, from early until late. In fact,
I have so much to do that I shall spend the
first three hours in prayer."

Martin Luther

Today's Prayer

*L*ord, sometimes teaching seems
like an overwhelming task. During
these difficult times, remind me that I
am working for a higher purpose:
Yours. Help me see beyond the struggle
of the moment. Whether today's work
seems easy or hard, help me to work
cheerfully, Lord, in a spirit of
celebration and determination, knowing
that when I work diligently and
prayerfully, I am working not only
for myself, but also for You.

Amen

22

Teach Me, Lord...
To Be
Compassionate

"Jesus went through all the towns
and villages, teaching in their
synagogues, preaching the good
news of the kingdom and healing
every disease and sickness. When he
saw the crowds, he had compassion
on them...."

Matthew 9:35,36

Teaching, on any level, has certain frustrations. From time to time, students misbehave, forget their lessons, disrupt the class, and ignore the teacher. In short, students have human frailties. Effective teachers establish discipline in the classroom, but at the same time, they model compassion.

I have known many compassionate teachers, and Pat Browning is consummate among them. For many years, Pat taught in public and private schools. She also teaches Sunday School and at one time was my mother's teacher. Pat always prepares well and lectures with clarity. But mostly she teaches compassion.

When my father died, Pat was there for my family. When my mother was very ill, Pat was steadfast. Pat brought love and soup, caring and conversation, smiles and encouragement. Most importantly, she brought herself.

On Saturdays, Pat calls members of her Sunday School class. Whether 10 or 100 are on her roll, she wants class members to know of her concern. Her compassion is crystal clear, as is the message of the One on whose behalf she calls.

"People don't care how much you know,
  until they know how much you care."

John Maxwell

"Beware that you are not swallowed up
  in books! An ounce of love is worth a
    pound of knowledge."

John Wesley

"He who is filled with love is filled with
    God Himself."

St. Augustine

Today's Prayer

*L*ord, help me to follow the example
of Your Son Jesus and fill me with
compassion. Use me according to Your
plan as a caring servant to those whom
I teach. And show me, Lord, ways to
translate my compassion into a
personal ministry that teaches Your
Word and glorifies Your name.

Amen

23

Teach Me, Lord...
To Be a
Bold Witness

"For God did not give us the spirit
of timidity, but a spirit of power, of
love and of self-discipline. So do not
be ashamed to testify about our
Lord...."

1 Timothy 1:7-8

When the message is true, the messenger should be bold. Jesus teaches us His truth will set us free. God offers His children a spirit of boldness and power so that they might proclaim the good news with unmistakable clarity.

We taught my daughter Julie to pray as soon as she was old enough to talk. Occasionally, she would agree to say the blessing when we dined at a restaurant. On one such occasion, I leaned over to Julie and softly asked if she would say a blessing for our meal. To my pleasure she agreed, no questions asked. But as I closed my eyes, I was startled to hear Julie shouting at the top of her lungs, "God is great; God is good. Let us thank him for our food. Amen."

I opened my eyes and, sure enough, everyone in the restaurant was looking our way. I could only chuckle because God had just taught me an important lesson through the blessing of my little Julie. She was un-ashamed to offer up a prayer for everyone to hear. And if a little child was unafraid to be bold, why then should I ever be timid in witnessing for my God?

So, with that lesson learned, let's all say it once more, this time with feeling: "God is great, God is good, let us thank him..." LOUDLY!

"Let God have perfect liberty when you speak.
Before God's message can liberate other souls,
the liberation must be real in you."

Oswald Chambers

"Take courage. We walk in the wilderness
today and in the Promised Land tomorrow."

D. L. Moody

"Ten thousand enemies cannot stop a Christian,
cannot even slow him down, if he meets them in
an attitude of complete trust in God."

A. W. Tozer

Today's Prayer

*L*ord, You love me so much You
sent Your Son to die on a cross for me.
Jesus took my shame and made it His.
Father, give me a childlike sense of
assurance in sharing the good news
of Your Message. May my witness be
bold and clear for all to hear.

Amen

24

Teach Me, Lord...
The Importance of
Your Wisdom

"Wisdom is supreme; therefore get
wisdom though it cost all you have,
Esteem her and she will exalt you;
embrace her, and she will honor you.
She will set a garland of grace on
your head and present you with a
crown of splendor."

Proverbs 4:7-9

The scriptures admonish us to seek after wisdom at all costs. To desire wisdom is to desire that which is incomparable (*Proverbs 8:11*). Teachers who share God's wisdom are like rare jewels (*Proverbs 20:15*).

Solomon, king of Israel and son of David, showed his love for the Lord by living righteously. The Lord appeared to Solomon in a dream desiring to grant Solomon a single wish. God was so pleased with Solomon's reply that He also granted Solomon what many of us would have wished for in the first place: riches and honor. What was the wish that so impressed God? Solomon asked God for wisdom.

Like King Solomon, we, too, must seek God's wisdom if we are to live righteous lives. As teachers, we not only seek wisdom, we share that wisdom with our students. The Bible teaches that wisdom begins with respect and love for our God. Perhaps Solomon learned this lesson from David who once wrote, "The fear of the LORD is the beginning of wisdom; all who follow his precepts have good understanding. To him belongs eternal praise" (*Psalm 111:10*). Christian teachers understand where wisdom begins, and they spread the word...more accurately, they spread *God's* Word.

"The doorstep to the temple of wisdom is
a knowledge of our own ignorance."

C. H. Spurgeon

"Knowledge is horizontal. Wisdom is vertical.
It comes down from above."

Billy Graham

"Don't expect wisdom to come into your life
like great chunks of rock on a conveyor
belt…Wisdom comes privately from God
as a byproduct of right decisions, godly
reactions, and the application of spiritual
principles to daily circumstances."

Chuck Swindoll

Today's Prayer

Lord, Grant me wisdom that I might know Your truth. As I come to know Your wisdom, grant me the ability to teach it with clarity and power. And Lord, may the truth that I teach transform my students so that they, too, might love and worship You as they obey Your Holy Word.

Amen

110

25

Teach Me, Lord...
To Love

"If I speak in the tongues of men
and angels, but have not love,
I am only a resounding gong or a
clanging cymbal."
I Corinthians 13:1

Great teaching, without love, is empty. Thus, teachers who seek to leave a lasting legacy must not only love the teaching profession, they must also love the people they teach.

Bill Anderson was Minister of Music at my church. He was also a great friend who often spoke of his love for my family and me. When my father died, I was unable to talk to Bill before I left town to be with my mother. A few days later, my mother and I arrived home from the visitation at the funeral home, and the telephone rang. Bill's voice came through loud and clear. I began to thank him for making a long distance call when he informed me that he and his wife, had just arrived in town. They had driven 14 hours.

When Bill and Jean came to the house a few minutes later, I expressed to them how stunned and grateful I was for their support. Bill responded, "We have told you that we love you, and now we wanted to show you." At that moment, I was reminded that our love for each other, like God's love for us, is expressed in deeds as well as words.

"Love is…a steady wish for the loved
person's ultimate good…."

C. S. Lewis

"Give me such love for God and men as
will blot out all hatred and bitterness."

Dietrich Bonhoeffer

"Inasmuch as love grows in you, so beauty grows.
For love is the beauty of the soul."

St. Augustine

Today's Prayer

Lord, help me love Your children more. You first loved me, and I can share that love with my students. May my teaching be filled with Your love, Lord, and may my students sense Your presence through the words that I speak and the actions that I take.

Amen

26

Teach Me, Lord...
To Endure

"He gives strength to the weary
and increases the power of the weak.
Even youths grow tired and weary
And young men stumble and fall;
But those who hope in the LORD
Will renew their strength.
They will soar like eagles;
They will run and not grow weary,
They will walk and not be faint."

Isaiah 40:29-31

Some days teaching seems like an endurance contest. Demands can be many. Students can be rowdy. Resources can be scarce. Some days it's tempting to retire from the classroom and leave the challenges to someone else. But Paul instructs us to do otherwise. In his letter to the Galatian church, he writes, "Let us not become weary in doing good, for at the proper time we will reap a harvest if we do not give up" (*Galatians 6:9*).

My first backpacking trip was not at all what I expected. Somehow visions of flat, flower-filled fields had permeated my imagination. Reality was quite different: a mountainous trail that seemed to go nowhere but up. My traveling companion, Don Franklin, an experienced backpacker, had simple advice: Don't keep staring at the far-away peak but instead put one foot in front of the other and keep walking. Don told me that soon enough, we would enjoy wonderful mountain vistas, and he was right. One step at a time, we reached the top. At the summit, we enjoyed breath-taking views, and we forgot about the agony of the climb.

Teaching is a marathon, not a sprint. Like a long journey up a mountain path, the climb has twists and turns. But if we prevail, we reach the peak. There, we discover what climbers and teachers have in common: the mountain-top experience.

"Keep adding, keep walking, keep advancing;
do not stop, do not turn back...."

St. Augustine

"All rising to a great place is by a winding stair."

Francis Bacon

"I learned as never before that persistent
calling upon the Lord breaks through every
stronghold of the devil, for nothing is impossible
with God. For Christians in these troubled
times, there is simply no other way."

Jim Cymbala

Today's Prayer

*L*ord, strengthen me. May my weakness be Your strength. When I grow tired, give me faith in myself and, more importantly, faith in You. Lord, help me to know that with You by my side, no journey is too long and no mountain is too steep. Keep me mindful, Lord, of the glorious victory that awaits those who put their undying trust in You.

Amen

27

Teach Me, Lord...
To Meditate on
Your Word

"Oh, how I love your law!
I meditate on it all day long.
Your commands make me wiser than my
enemies, for they are ever with me.
How sweet are your words to my taste,
sweeter than honey to my mouth!
I gain understanding from your precepts;
therefore I hate every wrong path.
Oh, how I love your law! I meditate on it
all day long."

Psalm 119:97,98,103,104

In The Message, Eugene Peterson translates the 119th Psalm in a conversational style. The following verses bear testimony to the life-changing power of God's instruction:.

"Oh, how I love all you've revealed;
    I reverently ponder it all the day long.
Your commands give me an edge on my enemies;
    They never become obsolete.
I've even become smarter than my teachers
    Since I've pondered and absorbed your counsel.
I've become wiser than the wise old sages
    Simply by doing what you tell me.
I watch my step, avoiding the ditches and ruts of evil
    So I can spend all my time keeping your Word.
I never make detours from the route you laid out;
    You gave me such good directions.
Your words are so choice, so tasty;
    I prefer them to the best home cooking.
With your instruction, I understand life;
    That's why I hate false propaganda."

Psalm 119:97-104 The Message

When we meditate on the teachings of God, we are transformed. And through this transformation, we grow as Christians and as teachers. As we come to a clearer understanding of God's word and His will, we can then share the wisdom that comes after many hours of quiet communion with God.

"The remedy for distractions is the same now
as it was in earlier and simpler times:
prayer, meditation and the cultivation of
the inner life."

A. W. Tozer

"God did not write a book and send it by
messenger to be read at a distance by
unaided minds. He spoke a Book and lives in
His spoken words, constantly speaking His
words and causing the power of them to persist
across the years."

A. W. Tozer

"O, let the place of secret prayer become to
me the most beloved spot on earth."

Andrew Murray

Today's Prayer

Lord, slow me down. Help me to
be still and know You are God. Help me
to take time each day to meditate on
Your Word. Lord, I know that
sometimes the urgent things of my life
crowd out the important things.
May I never feel too hurried to share
quiet time with You, Lord, for it is in
those quiet moments that I can best
sense Your love for me and
Your will for my life.

Amen

28

Teach Me, Lord...
To Trust
in You

"Whoever gives heed to instruction
prospers, and blessed is he who
trusts in the Lord."

Proverbs 16:20

God has big plans for teachers and students alike. He instructs them through His Holy Word and through His Spirit, but he also gives them free will to follow His instructions — or not. Those who trust God's Word will grow spiritually; those who ignore His teachings will stagnate.

It is the role of the Christian teacher to share the message that God is in control and that He is trustworthy. But to share that message in a genuine way, the Christian teacher must first trust God in all aspects of life.

The Psalmist writes, "In God have I put my trust: I will not be afraid what man can do unto me." (*Psalm 56:11 KJV*). When we study God's Word and seek His will in our lives, we, too, have nothing to fear. When we trust God completely, that trust is never betrayed. God is steadfast today, tomorrow, and forever.

"There is no other method of living piously and justly, than that of depending upon God."

John Calvin

"Never be afraid to trust an unknown future to a known God."

Corrie ten Boom

"Trust the past to God's mercy, the present to God's love, and the future to God's providence."

St. Augustine

"Attitude is all-important. Let the soul take a quiet attitude of faith and love toward God, and from there on, the responsibility is God's. He will make good on His commitments."

A. W. Tozer

Today's Prayer

*L*ord, I know that You have a plan
for my life, and I seek to follow Your will.
Show me Your purposes, Lord, and let
me always trust in You. When I am
fearful, give me courage. When I am
weak, let me lean upon Your strength
and Your Word. When I am headstrong,
Lord, forgive me and lead me back to
Your path that I might do Your work
and share Your Message today
and every day.

Amen

29

Teach Me, Lord...
To Be A Model
of Forgiveness

> "Blessed are the merciful,
> for they will be shown mercy."
>
> *Matthew 5:7*

Some students misbehave, and teachers must discipline those who do. But wise teachers don't stay angry for long, and they don't harbor grudges. Wise teachers understand the importance of forgiveness, and they teach the art of forgiveness to their students.

Jesus issues a stern warning: "For if you forgive men when they sin against you, your Heavenly Father will also forgive you. But if you do not forgive men their sins, your Father will not forgive your sins." (*Matthew 6:14-15*).

Teachers who seek to model Christ must become models of forgiveness. Forgiveness is not simply the right thing to do, it is a commandment of God. Those who bear grudges — whether teachers or students — do so at their own risk. But those who forgive completely and without resentment will be blessed — in this world *and* the next.

"We all agree that forgiveness is a beautiful
idea until we have to practice it."

C. S. Lewis

"Our Savior kneels down and gazes upon the
darkest acts of our lives. But rather than
recoil in horror, he reaches out in kindness
and says, 'I can clean that if you want.' And
from the basin of his grace, he scoops a palm
full of mercy and washes away our sin."

Max Lucado

"Forgiveness is God's command."

Martin Luther

Today's Prayer

Lord, thank You for the forgiveness
that You show me. I know that
forgiveness is Your commandment,
Lord, but sometimes forgiveness
is hard. Let me always be quick to
forgive others knowing that
I, too, seek to be forgiven.
And let me always be mindful of
Your son Jesus who loved all,
forgave all, and commanded us
to do the same.

Amen

30

Teach Me, Lord...
To Be
Patient

"A man's wisdom gives him
patience; it is to his glory to
overlook an offense."

Proverbs 19:11

Teaching is often an exercise in patience. But wise teachers never take daily frustrations too seriously. After all, patience is God's way.

In his first letter to the Thessalonians, Paul sends this message to the church: "We urge you, brethren, admonish the unruly, encourage the fainthearted, help the weak, be patient with everyone" (*1 Thessalonians 5:14 NASB*). As believers, Christian teachers must "admonish the unruly," but they must also "be patient with everyone," even uncooperative students.

When teachers exercise patience, they make life easier for themselves *and* their students. As Solomon writes in the book of Proverbs, patience results from wisdom. Thus, according to the Word of God, the wiser the teacher, the greater the teacher's patience.

"Patience is the companion of wisdom."

St. Augustine

"Christ alone can bring lasting peace —
peace with God — peace among men
and nations — and peace within our hearts."

Billy Graham

"It is the duty of every Christian to be
Christ to his neighbor."

Martin Luther

Today's Prayer

*L*ord, we live in an impatient world,
and amid the rush and struggle,
it is easy to lose sight of Your grace.
Give me a patient heart and an
understanding mind, Lord. Your Word
tells me to be patient with Your
children, but sometimes patience is
difficult. Help me to love more,
to worry less, and to rediscover each
day the peace that comes when I
patiently follow Your will.

Amen

Teach Me, Lord...
To Enjoy Teaching

"I thank my God every time I
remember you. In all my prayers for
all of you, I always pray with joy
because of your partnership in the
gospel from the first day until now,
being confident of this, that he who
began a good work in you will carry
it on to completion until the day of
Christ Jesus."

Philippians 1:3-6

The Apostle Paul was joyful as he remembered his students at Philippi. He had established the church and had taught the tenets of the Christian faith to the Philippians. Paul and the Philippians had become partners in spiritual growth, and now, Paul was sure that the church would grow. As Paul remembered and prayed for his friends, he was filled with joy.

Annie Sullivan was Helen Keller's teacher. She, like Paul, discovered the joys of teaching under the most difficult of circumstances. Sullivan was employed by the Keller family to tutor Helen, a young girl who was both deaf and blind. Not surprisingly, the tutoring process went slowly at first. But one day, Sullivan made an important breakthrough with her pupil. Soon afterward, Anne wrote these words in her journal, "My heart is singing with joy this morning. A miracle has happened! The light of understanding has shone upon my little pupil's mind, and, behold, all things are changed."

Teachers are blessed when their students have flashes of insight. These "aha" moments can be thrilling for students and teachers alike. Wise teachers savor these moments while giving humble thanks to the One whose hand guides all.

"The ability to rejoice in any situation is
a sign of spiritual maturity."

Billy Graham

"It is only with gratitude that life becomes rich."

Dietrich Bonhoeffer

Today's Prayer

Lord, we live in an impatient world,
and amid the rush and struggle, it is
easy to lose sight of Your grace.
Give me a joyful heart and an
understanding mind, Lord. Your Word
tells me to be patient with Your
children, but sometimes patience is
difficult. Help me to love more,
to worry less, and to rediscover each
day the peace that comes when I
joyously follow Your will.

Amen

Scripture Verses
for Teachers

> "Feed the flock of God which is
> among you..."
>
> *1 Peter 5:2 KJV*

Great Teachers Offer
Great Encouragement to Their Students

"But encourage one another day after day,
as long as it is still called "Today," so that
none of you will be hardened by the
deceitfulness of sin."

Hebrews 3:13 NASB

"Let the word of Christ dwell in you richly
in all wisdom; teaching and admonishing
one another in psalms and hymns and
spiritual songs, singing with grace
in your hearts to the Lord."

Colossians 3:16 KJV

"Be kindly affectioned one to another with
brotherly love; in honor preferring one
another; not slothful in business; fervent in
spirit; serving the Lord; rejoicing in hope;
patient in tribulation; continuing
instant in prayer...."

Romans 12:10-12 KJV

"...I tell you the truth, whatever you did for
one of the least of these brothers of mine,
you did for me."

Matthew 25:40 NIV

Wise Teachers Cultivate Cheerfulness in Themselves and Their Students

---

"...the cheerful heart has a continual feast."

Proverbs 15:15 NIV

"A cheerful heart is good medicine, but
a crushed spirit dries up the bones."

Proverbs 17:22 NIV

"Delight thyself also in the LORD; and
he shall give thee the desires of thine heart."

Psalm 37:4 KJV

"Verily, verily, I say unto you, Whatsoever
ye shall ask the Father in my name, he will
give it you. Hitherto have ye asked nothing in
my name: ask, and ye shall receive,
that your joy may be full."

John 16:23-24 KJV

"Joy I will thank you, Lord with all my heart;
I will tell of all the marvelous things you have
done. I will be filled with joy because of you;
I will sing praises to your name, O Most High."

Psalm 9: 1-2 NLT

"The fear of the Lord is the beginning of
knowledge, but fools despise wisdom
and discipline."

Proverbs 1:7 NIV

"He who heeds discipline shows the way to life,
but whoever ignores correction
leads others astray."

Proverbs 10:17 NIV

"But the love of the Lord remains forever with
those who fear him. His salvation extends to
the children's children of those who are
faithful to his covenant, of those who
obey his commandments!"

Psalm 103:17-18 NLT

"Whoever gives heed to instruction prospers,
and blessed is he that trusts in the Lord."

Proverbs 16:20 NIV

"Do not despise the Lord's discipline and
do not resent his rebuke, because
the Lord disciplines those he loves,
as a father the son he delights in."

Proverbs 3:11-12 NIV

*Christian Teachers Share the Message
of God's Everlasting Love...*

"For God so loved the world, that he gave
his only begotten Son, that whosoever
believeth in him should not perish,
but have everlasting life."

John 3:16 KJV

"The Lord says, 'I will rescue those who love me.
I will protect those who trust in my name.'"

Psalm 91:14 NLT

"For I am persuaded, that neither death,
nor life, nor angels, nor principalities, nor
powers, nor things present, nor things to come,
nor height, nor depth, nor any other creature,
shall be able to separate us from the love of God,
which is in Christ Jesus our Lord."

Romans 8:38-39 KJV

"For the Lord is good. His unfailing love
continues forever, and his faithfulness
continues to each generation."

Psalm 100:5 NLT

Christian Teachers Cultivate a Spirit of Forgiveness in Themselves and Their Students

---

"Be ye therefore merciful, as your Father
also is merciful."

Luke 6:36 KJV

"A man's wisdom gives him patience;
it is to his glory to overlook an offense."

Proverbs 19:11 NIV

"Then came Peter to him, and said,
Lord, how oft shall my brother sin
against me, and I forgive him?
till seven times? Jesus saith unto him,
I say not unto thee, Until seven times:
but, Until seventy times seven."

Matthew 18:21-22 KJV

"So in everything, do to others what you
would have them do to you, for this
sums up the Law and the Prophets."

Matthew 7:12 NIV

"Blessed are the merciful:
for they shall obtain mercy."

Matthew 5:7 KJV

"Trust in the LORD with all thine heart;
and lean not unto thine own understanding.
In all thy ways acknowledge him, and
he shall direct thy paths."

Proverbs 3:5-6 KJV

"And all things are of God, who hath
reconciled us to himself by Jesus Christ,
and hath given to us the ministry of
reconciliation...."

II Corinthians 5:18 KJV

"Teach me to do thy will; for thou art my God:
thy Spirit is good; lead me into
the land of uprightness."

Psalm 143:10 KJV

"For whosoever shall do the will of my Father
which is in heaven, the same is my brother,
and sister, and mother."

Matthew 12:50 KJV

"...Father, if it be possible, let this cup pass
from me: nevertheless, not as I will,
but as thou wilt."

Matthew 26:39 KJV

Wise Teachers Share The Message
That Each Day is God's Gift

"This is the day the Lord has made;
  let us rejoice and be glad in it."

Psalm 118:24 NIV

"...let the hearts of those who seek the Lord
  rejoice. Look to the Lord and his strength;
  seek his face always."

I Chronicles 16:10-11 NIV

"The Lord is king! Let the earth rejoice!
  Let the farthest islands be glad."

Psalm 97:1 NLT

"These things I have spoken unto you, that
  in me ye might have peace. In the world
ye shall have tribulation: but be of good cheer;
  I have overcome the world."

John 16:33 KJV

"It is good to give thanks to the Lord,
  to sing praises to the Most High. It is good
to proclaim your unfailing love in the morning,
  your faithfulness in the evening."

Psalm 92:2-3 NLT

On Trusting God's Plans

"The steps of a good man are ordered by
the LORD...."

Psalm 37:23 KJV

"In his heart a man plans his course,
but the Lord determines his steps."

Proverbs 16:9 NIV

"Every plant that my Father has not planted
will be pulled up by the roots."

Matthew 15:13 NIV

"O the depth of the riches both of the
wisdom and knowledge of God!
How unsearchable are his judgments,
and his ways past finding out!
For who hath known the mind of the Lord?
or who hath been his counselor?"

Romans 11:33-34 KJV

"Thou, Lord, in the beginning hast laid the
foundation of the earth; and the heavens
are the works of thine hands."

Hebrews 1:10 KJV

During Difficult Times, Christian Teachers Help Their Students Seek God's Healing Hand

---

"Then they cried unto the LORD
in their trouble, and he saved them
out of their distresses."

Psalm 107:13 KJV

"He heals the brokenhearted,
and binds their wounds."

Psalm 147:3 NASB

"I tell you the truth, you will weep and mourn
while the world rejoices. You will grieve,
but your grief will turn to joy."

John 16:20 NIV

"He restoreth my soul: he leadeth me in
the paths of righteousness
for his name's sake."

Psalm 23:3 KJV

"The LORD is my rock, and my fortress, and
my deliverer; my God, my strength,
in whom I will trust..."

Psalm 18:2 KJV

"Therefore do not worry about tomorrow,
for tomorrow will worry about itself.
Each day has enough trouble of its own."

Matthew 6:34 NIV

"Yea, though I walk through the valley of the
shadow of death, I will fear no evil: for
thou art with me; thy rod and
thy staff they comfort me."

Psalm 23:4 KJV

"Cast your burden upon the Lord and
He will sustain you: He will never allow
the righteous to be shaken."

Psalm 55:22 NASB

"Trust in him at all times, O people;
pour out your hearts to him,
for God is our refuge."

Psalm 62:8 NIV

"Daughter, be of good comfort;
thy faith hath made thee whole."

Matthew 9:24 KJV

Wise Teachers Understand the Need for Patience and the Futility of Anger

---

"A patient man has great understanding,
but a quick-tempered man displays folly."

Proverbs 14:29 NIV

"But I tell you that anyone who is angry
with his brother is subject to judgment."

Matthew 5:22 NIV

"Make no friendship with an angry man...."

Proverbs 22:24 KJV

"Refrain from anger and turn from wrath;
do not fret — it leads only to evil."

Psalm 37:8 NIV

"....do not let the sun go down on your anger,
and do not give the devil an opportunity."

Ephesians 4:26-27 NASB

"And the servant of the Lord must not strive;
but be gentle unto all men, apt to teach,
patient; in meekness instructing those that
oppose themselves ..."

II Timothy 2:24-25 KJV

Christian Teachers Share
God's Saving Message

"You are the light of the world. A city on a
hill cannot be hidden. Neither do people
light a lamp and put it under a bowl. Instead
they put it on its stand, and it gives light to
everyone in the house. In the same way,
let your light shine before men, that they
may see your good deeds and praise
your Father in heaven."

Matthew 5:14-16 NIV

"As you go, preach this message:
'The kingdom of heaven is near.'"

Matthew 10:7 NIV

"The fruit of the righteous is a tree of life;
and he that winneth souls is wise."

Proverbs 11:30 KJV

"And Jesus said unto them, Come ye after me,
and I will make you to become fishers of men.
And straightway they forsook their nets,
and followed him."

Mark 1:17-18 KJV

"Now then we are ambassadors for Christ...."

II Corinthians 5:20 KJV

Index

"He who listens to a life-giving
rebuke will be at home
among the wise."

Proverbs 15:31 NIV

About the Author

Jim Gallery lives and writes in Middle Tennessee. He serves as publisher for both Brighton Books and Walnut Grove Press. In addition, Jim is a sought-after speaker and lecturer. He has over 20 year's experience as a pastor.

Jim is a graduate of the University of South Florida and the New Orleans Baptist Theological Seminary. He is the father of two children, Julie and Jimmy.

Some of his other titles include:

God Can Handle It
God Can Handle It... Teenagers
God Can Handle It... Fathers
Prayers of a Godly Woman
Prayers of a Righteous Man